# Strawberry Fair

## Quilts with a Country Flair

ELIZABETH HAMBY CARLSON

*Martingale*®
& COMPANY

## Acknowledgments

Many thanks to:

Mary Green, Karen Soltys, and all the staff
at Martingale for their help and enthusiasm;

Betsy, Dolores, and Jean for all their welcome advice,
opinions, and especially encouragement;

Sheri Flemming for beautiful machine quilting;

My husband, Ken, for his help and support whenever I need it.

## Credits

President: Nancy J. Martin
CEO: Daniel J. Martin
Publisher: Jane Hamada
Editorial Director: Mary V. Green
Managing Editor: Tina Cook
Technical Editor: Ellen Pahl
Copy Editor: Durby Peterson
Design Director: Stan Green
Illustrator: Brian Metz
Cover and Text Designer: Regina Girard
Photographer: Brent Kane

That Patchwork Place® is an imprint
of Martingale & Company®.

Strawberry Fair: Quilts with a Country Flair
© 2005 by Elizabeth Hamby Carlson

Martingale & Company
20205 144th Avenue NE
Woodinville, WA 98072-8478 USA
www.martingale-pub.com

Printed in China
10 09 08 07 06 05          8 7 6 5 4 3 2 1

## Mission Statement
Dedicated to providing quality products and service to inspire creativity.

**Library of Congress Cataloging-in-Publication Data**
Carlson, Elizabeth Hamby.
  Strawberry fair: quilts with a country flair /
Elizabeth Hamby Carlson.
    p. cm.
  Includes bibliographical references.
  ISBN 1-56477-524-0
  1. Appliqué—Patterns. 2. Quilting. 3. Album quilts.
4. Strawberries in art. I. Title.
  TT779.C369 2005
  746.46'041—dc22

                               2004025048

# Contents

## Strawberry Fair

*As I was going to Strawberry Fair,*
*Singing, singing, buttercups and daisies,*
*I met a maiden taking her wares, fol-de-dee.*
*Her eyes were blue and golden her hair,*
*As she went on to Strawberry Fair.*

*"Kind sir, pray pick of my basket," she said,*
*Singing, singing, buttercups and daisies,*
*"My cherries ripe or my roses red, fol-de-dee.*
*My strawberries sweet I can of them spare,*
*As I go on to Strawberry Fair."*

*—Traditional English folk song*

Just as most of us have a favorite color, we often have a favorite thing we like to collect in all sorts of versions. One friend of mine likes anything with kittens; another friend likes things with cows. For me, it has always been strawberries. Fabric, wrapping paper, wallpaper, dishes (lots of dishes), almost anything adorned with a strawberry motif calls out to me. Over the years, friends and family who know this have added to my collection with pincushions, jewelry, and assorted pictures and prints. One of my favorites is a picture postcard of a pair of needlepoint slippers with glowing red strawberries and white blossoms on a navy background, given as a Christmas gift in 1858 to Queen Victoria. My friend and traveling companion on a trip to England saw the slippers in a London museum on a day when I was too ill to leave the hotel; knowing I would like them, she brought me the postcard as a memento. One day I hope to get to the museum and see the Queen's slippers in person! My own enthusiasm for needlework has led me to stitch lots of strawberries in needlepoint, crewel, cross-stitch, and of course appliqué.

In 1989, I made a miniature Baltimore Album quilt and enjoyed the process so much that I decided to make another miniature album quilt, this time filled

*Strawberry Fair, 31" x 31"*
*Hand appliquéd and quilted by*
*Elizabeth Hamby Carlson, 1993*

with strawberry designs. The quilt's name was taken from the traditional English folk song "Strawberry Fair."

Many of the first 6" Strawberry Fair quilt blocks were inspired by my strawberry-themed collection. An English enamel box—itself inspired by an eighteenth-century strawberry-printed cotton fabric—provided a color palette for the quilt. I adapted the block designs from, among other things, a nineteenth-century theorem painting, a collection of fruit motifs by a seventeenth-century London print seller, and a fabric designed by William Morris. Appliqué ideas are everywhere, once you start looking for them.

A decade or so after making my first Strawberry Fair quilt, I revised the pattern and made a new, larger version. The new quilt, "Strawberry Fair Album" on page 34, was the starting point for this collection of quilts and other small projects. If you share my enthusiasm for berries and blossoms, I hope one or more of these patterns will entice you to go a-berrying too.

# Quiltmaking Techniques

This section covers basic quilting and appliqué techniques. Instructions for individual quilt projects will refer you back to specific techniques as needed to complete the quilt.

## Tools and Supplies

Having and using the right tool for the job is one of the keys to success in any project. Here are some of the tools I rely on to make quiltmaking easy, fun, and successful.

**Sewing machine:** Your sewing machine needs to be in good working order, with even tension and a good straight stitch for accurate piecing. A quilter's ¼" presser foot is especially helpful for machine piecing. For machine appliqué you need a machine that does a zigzag stitch or a buttonhole stitch. To do mock hand appliqué, the machine needs to have an adjustable blind hemstitch.

**Rotary-cutting equipment:** This consists of a trio of tools—a rotary cutter, mat, and ruler. Use a rotary cutter with a good sharp blade. When the blade is dull or nicked, the fabric layers are not cut cleanly. A rotary mat with grid lines will help you keep fabrics square when cutting, but do not use the grid lines for measuring. Always measure with your ruler.

You will need a rotary ruler with both vertical and horizontal measuring lines. I find that a 6" x 24" ruler is a good size for most uses. A large, square rotary ruler is also very handy for squaring up blocks.

**Needles:** Put a fresh needle in your machine when you start your quilt. For piecing, use size 70/10 or 75/11. For machine appliqué, use the needle size suggested for the appliqué method you have chosen.

Hand appliqué needles need to be long, thin, and flexible. My favorites are size 11 straw needles for needle-turn appliqué and size 11 Sharps for any appliqué where the edges are turned under before the pieces are positioned on the background.

For hand quilting, use short, fairly stiff needles called Betweens. Size 10 is my favorite.

**Thread:** For machine piecing I use 50-weight, 100%-cotton sewing thread in a neutral color. Light to medium gray seems to blend well with most fabrics. If your fabrics are very dark, use darker thread. Machine appliqué can be done with a wide variety of threads. For mock hand appliqué I use nylon invisible thread, size .004 for the top thread only. This thread is very fine, easy to work with, and available in either clear or smoke color. Use the smoke for darker fabrics. I suggest a 50-weight thread for the bobbin, in a color that matches the background fabric. For fusible appliqué I use a 50-weight, 100%-cotton thread that matches the appliqué fabric. If you want the stitch to have a more decorative look, use heavier thread in a contrasting color.

Thread for hand appliqué should match the color of the appliqué piece so the stitches will be nearly invisible. Use 100%-cotton thread, cotton-wrapped polyester, or silk. If you have difficulty threading the fine needles, look for a needle threader made for use with fine needles.

To quilt, use 100%-cotton thread made specifically for hand or machine quilting. Quilting thread is coated with a light glaze that makes it less likely to tangle.

**Stiletto:** A stiletto (or a small screwdriver) is helpful to guide pieces under the presser foot, ease fabric, and adjust seam allowances that want to flip the wrong way. The tip of the stiletto can go where your fingers can not, and should not!

**Scissors:** For cutting fabric appliqués you'll need small, sharp scissors that cut cleanly, right to the tip. Reserve your appliqué scissors for fabric only. Use another pair of small scissors for cutting freezer paper and plastic templates.

**Light table:** Use a light table or light box when tracing the appliqué pattern onto background fabric or when placing appliqué pieces on an unmarked background block. Portable light tables, designed for quilters, are available in many quilt shops.

**Freezer paper:** Ordinary freezer paper, found at the grocery store, is ideal for appliqué templates.

When pressed onto fabric, the plastic coating causes the paper to adhere, but it is easily removed and leaves no residue.

🐚 **Tracing paper:** When you need to reverse an appliqué pattern, trace it first onto tracing paper. When the tracing paper is turned to the other side you will be able to see the pattern clearly, and it will be reversed.

🐚 **Paper-backed fusible web:** There are many brands of fusible web available. Choose one that is lightweight so your quilt will not be stiff. I prefer to use fusible web sold in paper-sized sheets rather than on a roll because sheets are easier to store flat.

🐚 **Glue stick:** A glue stick is helpful for holding appliqué shapes and seam allowances in place while you stitch. The glue stick must be water soluble so the glue will rinse out of the appliqué block in cold water when you are finished. Try different brands until you find one that works well for you, and always test a new brand before using it in your appliqué.

🐚 **Fine-line permanent-ink pens:** Use these pens for adding small details to your appliquéd blocks. I like to use Pigma pens, which are available in several colors. Before using it on your quilt, test the pen to make sure the ink is permanent.

🐚 **Embroidery floss:** Some of the appliqué projects include embroidered details. Use 100%-cotton embroidery floss. The six-strand floss can be divided as suggested in the embroidery stitch directions. See "Embroidery" on page 15.

🐚 **Orange stick:** This thin wooden stick with a beveled tip (similar to the tip of a screwdriver) is normally used by manicurists but is very handy for glue-stick appliqué as well. I use one to hold little pieces in place while applying glue, to pick up glue-covered pieces, and to turn the edges of appliqué pieces over the edges of freezer-paper templates.

🐚 **Lap pillow:** Using a lap pillow for hand sewing is a trick I learned from one of my students. The pillow elevates the work a bit and provides a place to rest my hands and smooth my block. I can pin little pieces on it to keep track of them. My pillow measured 12" x 18" before stuffing, and it is stuffed very hard. It has a plain muslin top that doesn't distract from whatever work I have on it. The lady who made my pillow embroidered it with the words "my third hand," and it really is just that.

# Cutting and Piecing

All of the projects in this book are designed for rotary cutting and are easily pieced by machine. Cutting patchwork pieces with a rotary cutter is faster and more accurate than cutting them with scissors. Use your cutter to cut appliqué blocks and borders as well as the patchwork strips and pieces in your project.

## Cutting Straight Strips

Directions are given for right-hand cutting. Reverse directions if you are left-handed.

1. Fold and press the fabric with the selvages aligned. Fabric should be flat with no wrinkles or puckers.

2. Place the folded fabric on the cutting mat with the fold closest to you. Align a square ruler so that the ruler's horizontal lines are parallel to the folded edge. Place a 6" x 24" ruler alongside the left-hand edge of the square ruler.

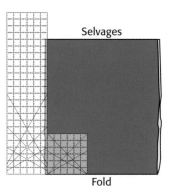

Selvages

Fold

3. Remove the square ruler and make a rotary cut along the right edge of the cutting ruler to straighten the edge.

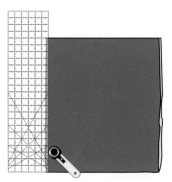

4. Place the cutting ruler on the fabric, lining up the newly cut edge with the ruler marking for the desired strip width. Cut strips as needed and make another straightening cut every 6" or so.

## Cutting Background Squares

1. Place a square ruler on the fabric and cut the first two sides of the square.

2. Turn the fabric around and line up the newly cut edges with the appropriate measurement on the ruler. Cut the remaining two sides of the square.

## Squaring Up Blocks

After you've finished stitching the appliqués on the background square, you need to square up the block, keeping the design centered. To square up an appliqué block, line up the vertical and horizontal centerlines of the block with the centerlines of the desired size square on the ruler. For example, the center line of a 10½" square is the 5¼" line. Cut the first two sides of the square. Turn the block around and cut the other two sides.

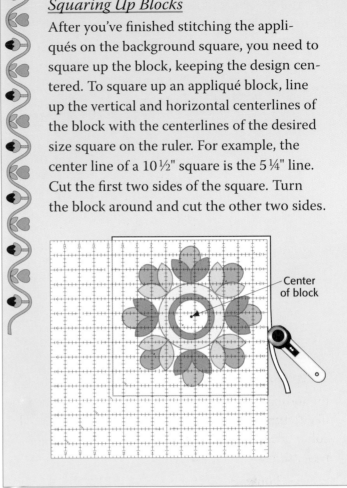

Center of block

## Sewing Accurate Seams

The success of your quilt depends on accurate sewing and consistent ¼" seams. In my classes, I help students set up their machines with a seam guide; they are amazed at the improvement in their accuracy. Make a seam guide for your machine and sew a set of test strips following these steps.

1. Place either ¼" graph paper or the ¼" mark on a rotary ruler directly under the needle on your machine. Lower the needle until it pierces the ¼" line on the graph paper or just touches the marking on the ruler. Make sure the ruler or paper is straight by aligning a horizontal line on the machine with a horizontal line on the ruler or graph paper. (The edge of the throat plate makes a good guide.) Then lower the presser foot to hold it in place.

2. Right along the edge of the ruler or paper, just in front of the feed dogs and exactly ¼" to the right of the needle, stack several pieces of 1" long masking tape.

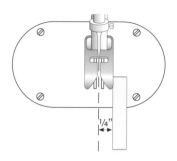

3. Check the accuracy of your seam guide with three test strips, two dark and one light, cut 1½" wide. Sew two of the strips together. The distance from the cut edge to the sewing line should be ¼". If it's not, repeat steps 1 and 2 to readjust the masking tape guide. When the seam allowance and stitching line measure exactly ¼", press the seam toward the darker fabric.

4. Sew the remaining strip to the light strip. Press the new seam allowances away from the light strip. If the seam allowances are accurate, the center strip will now measure 1".

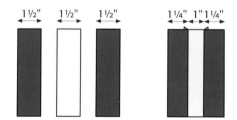

## Pressing

Pressing is planned so that seam allowances will oppose one another when you sew the blocks and rows together. Pay close attention to the pressing directions provided with each project; they are important!

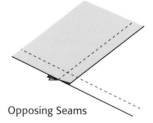

Opposing Seams

# Appliqué

There are so many ways to appliqué—both by hand and by machine. Being familiar with many different appliqué methods is like having a good assortment of tools in your toolbox. When getting ready to start an appliqué project, you can choose which tool or appliqué method is best for the project at hand. If a quilt is to be a very special heirloom quilt, hand appliqué is always my first choice. Not every quilt is meant to be an heirloom though, and for quilts that will receive hard wear, or for simple seasonal projects, machine appliqué is often the best and most efficient choice. In this section I've included directions for several of my own favorite hand and machine methods. Choose one of these, or the appliqué method you like best, to appliqué your *Strawberry Fair* projects.

## Preparing Background Fabric

Background blocks for appliqué should be cut carefully so that the sides of the block are parallel to the lengthwise grain. When the blocks are set together in the quilt, the lengthwise grain should run consistently from top to bottom so the finished quilt will lie or hang flat and square.

As you work on the block, it may fray and pieces may shift, so the background blocks are cut oversize. When the block is finished, trim and square it up to the measurement indicated in the project directions, referring to "Squaring Up Blocks" on page 7.

### Mark the Grain
Mark the lengthwise grain with a small arrow near the edge of the background blocks as you cut them, so you'll be able to keep the blocks in the correct orientation in the quilt.

An easy way to place the appliqué pieces on the background blocks is to use a light table. Once you've traced or copied the pattern from the book, place it on the light table and lay the background block over it, carefully matching centerlines. Position the appliqués on the block, pinning if necessary. Pay careful attention to the stitching order marked on the pattern.

## Hand Appliqué Stitch

The traditional appliqué stitch is the same for all the hand appliqué methods. Stitches should be small, even, and nearly invisible.

1. Use a single strand of thread in a color that closely matches the appliqué. Hide the starting knot on the back of the appliqué, in the fold made by the seam allowance. Bring the needle through the folded edge of the appliqué.

2. Make the first stitch into the background fabric, just under the edge of the appliqué and below the spot where the needle emerged. The thread does not travel forward or backward on the front of the block but goes straight down off the appliqué.

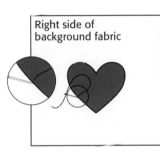

Right side of background fabric

3. Run the needle not more than ⅛" under the background fabric, parallel to the edge of the appliqué. Bring the needle up through the background fabric, catching one or two threads on the folded edge of the appliqué.

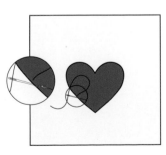

On the front, all you see is a tiny dot of thread where each stitch is taken, while on the back, the thread runs almost parallel to the appliqué edge. To end the stitching, take two stitches behind the appliqué, close to the stitching line. Bring the

needle through the loop of thread before you draw it up tight. Then clip the thread.

Wrong side of background fabric

4. Inside points need special attention. As you near an inside point, make your stitches even closer together. At the point of the V, take a deeper bite into the appliqué fabric; bring the needle out three or four threads inside the folded edge. Take two or three stitches at the V, right next to each other, almost like a satin stitch. As you stitch away from the point, continue to keep your stitches very close together.

5. Outside points need to be secured to prevent fraying. When stitching toward an outside point, take very small stitches to keep any stray threads or frayed edges out of sight. Stitch up one side, right to the point, and take one stitch that comes up inside the appliqué, several threads in from the point, to secure it. Fold under the seam allowance at the point first, and then fold under the seam allowance on the other side of the point. Sew down the other side with tiny stitches.

Tuck seam allowance under leaf point with needle.

6. To layer one piece on top of another, leave the bottom piece flat where it will be overlaid—do not turn under any seam allowances. Sew the top piece to the bottom piece, stitching only through the bottom piece. Try not to catch the background fabric in your stitch.

## Template-Free Needle-Turn Appliqué

This easy method is the one I used for making the blocks for "Strawberry Fair Album" on page 34.

1. Lay the background fabric, wrong side up, over the master appliqué pattern, matching centers. With a sharp pencil, trace the appliqué pattern onto the wrong side of the background fabric. If the appliqué pattern is asymmetrical, you must reverse the pattern before tracing it onto the background block. Reverse the pattern by tracing it onto tracing paper first, then turn the paper over and trace from the back side of the tracing paper onto the background fabric.

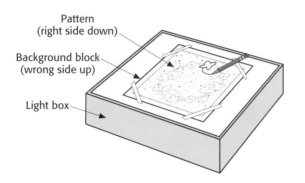

2. Follow the letters and numbers indicating the order in which the pieces are to be stitched. For this method you must stitch the bottommost pieces first. This usually means that stems are stitched first, and then leaves, flowers, and so forth.

3. Place the first piece of appliqué fabric, right side up, onto the right side of the background fabric so the appliqué fabric extends at least ½" beyond the lines of the appliqué shape drawn on the wrong side of the background. Pin the fabric in place if necessary. Turn the block to the wrong side and hand baste the appliqué and background fabrics together with a running stitch, exactly on the traced line. Use heavy thread, such as quilting thread, and a thick needle with a large eye (embroidery or crewel needles work well) to sew the running stitch. Running stitches should not be longer than ¼" and should be shorter on tight curves and near points. Do not knot the basting thread. The basted line will be your turn-under

line for the appliqué. Do not baste areas that will be overlaid by another appliqué piece; these areas will be left flat.

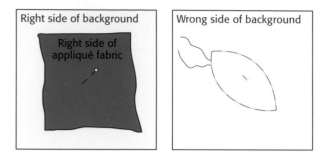

4. Trim the appliqué fabric to a ⅛" seam allowance outside the basted line.

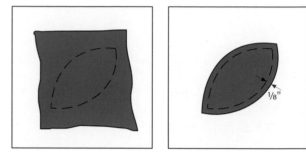

5. For large pieces, or long stems, do not trim the entire seam allowance at once. Trim short lengths as you go. Snip the thread and remove the basting stitches from the trimmed section. Begin on a gentle curve when possible; appliqué, turning under the seam allowance with your needle as you go. Because the turning line has been "perforated" with the heavy thread and needle, the seam allowance will turn under easily, right on the line, just like magic! Turn under just a little bit at a time on curves, using a sweeping motion to smooth the seam allowance underneath. Continue stitching, trimming the seam allowance, and removing basting as you go.

## Freezer-Paper Appliqué

To baste seam allowances under before appliquéing, I often use glue instead of thread. With this method you can prepare all the pieces for the block and preview them before stitching. This method is good for small-scale appliqué and is the method I used for "English Floral Sampler" on page 64.

1. Make freezer-paper templates by tracing each appliqué piece onto the dull side of the freezer paper. Use a fine line permanent-ink pen for tracing. Cut out the paper templates right on the marked line.

   **Note:** If the pattern is directional or asymmetrical, reverse the templates as in step 1 of "Template-Free Needle-Turn Appliqué" on page 10.

2. Place the freezer-paper templates on the wrong side of the appliqué fabric with the dull side of the paper up. Leave room for a ³⁄₁₆" seam allowance around each piece. Place shapes with points, such as leaves, so that the points are on the bias. This technique will make turning the seam allowance easier. If there is a motif in the fabric you wish to feature, feel free to ignore the grain line.

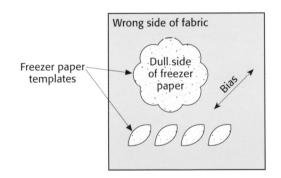

3. Press with a hot, dry iron; the shiny side of the freezer paper will adhere to the fabric.

4. Cut out the fabric shape, leaving a ³⁄₁₆" seam allowance all around the piece.

5. With the appliqué pieces flat and wrong side up, run the end of the glue stick over the seam allowance of each piece. On small pieces, the glue may cover the entire piece. Do not glue an edge that will lie under another piece, because that edge will not need to be basted. It is easier to turn under the seam allowances after the glue has dried for several minutes; you can glue many pieces at once and then go back and turn the seam allowances under.

6. After applying the glue, clip the seam allowances on inside curves and inside points to within one or two threads from the paper.

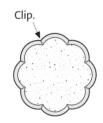

Clip.

7. Using either your fingers or a wooden orange stick, fold the fabric over the edge of the paper. Fold only a small bit of fabric at a time. On outside curves, make tiny pleats as you would when crimping a piecrust. Once you have achieved a smooth edge, flatten the seam allowance into little pleats on the back.

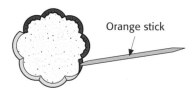

Orange stick

8. For leaves and other pieces with outside points, fold one edge of the fabric leaf over the template, extending the fold beyond the points of the paper on each end. Fold the other side in the same way. The leaf will have smooth curves and sharp points, with a little "flag" of fabric sticking out at each end. Fold the flags behind each point and press with your fingers. There will probably be enough glue to hold the flags in place. If not, leave them sticking out for now. You can push them behind the point with your needle when you appliqué the piece to the background.

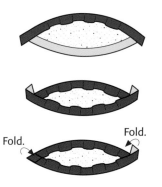

Fold.       Fold.

9. Stitch the appliqué pieces to the background block using the traditional appliqué stitch. See "Hand Appliqué Stitch" on page 9.

10. When the appliqué is complete, carefully make a snip in the background fabric behind each appliqué to expose the paper template. Do not cut

within ⅛" of the stitching line. The opening should be just big enough to remove the freezer paper.

Wrong side of background block

11. Soak the block in cold clear water for at least 10 minutes to rinse out the glue and soften the paper. Take the block from the water and carefully remove the paper from each piece with tweezers. Rinse the block again in fresh cold water. Roll it in a thick white towel and blot, removing as much moisture as possible to prevent bleeding. Lay the block flat to dry.

12. When the block is completely dry, steam press it from the wrong side, placing a thick white towel under the block to avoid crushing the appliqué.

### Appliqué Hint

Some quilters cut away the background fabric behind appliqués and others don't. It is a matter of personal preference. If the appliqué shape is large, and I will be quilting it, I cut away the background to avoid quilting through an extra layer of fabric.

## Stems and Vines

Narrow stems and vines may be easily appliquéd without templates. One good way is discussed in "Template-Free Needle-Turn Appliqué" on page 10. Just baste the stem fabric to the background block and appliqué as you would any other piece. There are also several ways to make stems from bias strips. Here are two methods I use.

## Needle-Turn Bias Stems

A bias strip cut ½" wide will make a very narrow stem, ⅛" to 3/16" wide. If you want a wider stem, cut the bias strip wider. For example, if you want a ¼" finished stem, cut the bias strip ¾" wide.

1. Rotary cut a bias strip of stem fabric ½" wide (or the width you prefer). I usually don't bother to measure the length precisely; I just cut plenty and trim as needed.

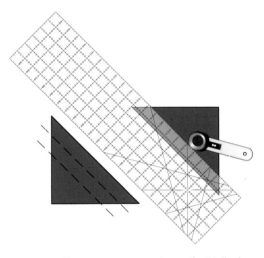

2. Press a seam allowance approximately 3/16" along one long edge.

### Pressing Hint

Don't use a high steam setting when pressing the bias strips, and keep your fingers ahead of the iron. The strips will fold easily once you get them started.

3. Attach the stem by appliquéing the folded edge in place; then stitch the other side, turning under the raw edge with the needle as you go. If the stem is curved, stitch the folded edge on the inside curve first.

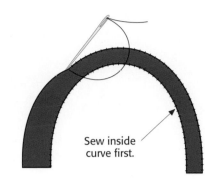

Sew inside curve first.

## Bias-Bar Stems

Bias bars are long, thin metal or plastic strips sold especially for making bias stems. They come in a variety of widths.

1. Cut a bias strip of stem fabric slightly more than four times the width of the finished stem. Fold and press the strip in half, wrong sides together.

2. Machine sew the stem so that the distance from the stitched line to the folded edge is the same as the finished width of the stem. For example, if you want a ¼"-wide stem, stitch ¼" from the folded edge. Trim the seam allowance to ⅛" after stitching.

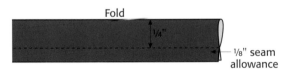

Fold
¼"
⅛" seam allowance

3. Slide a plastic or metal bias bar the width of the finished stem into the pocket made by the stitching. Adjust the stem so that the seam is centered on the back of the bias bar; press with the bias bar still inside. The bias bars will withstand the heat of the iron. Slide them along the length of the bias and continue pressing as needed.

Bias bar

4. Wait a moment for the bias bar to cool off, and then remove it from the stem. Press the stem flat. It is now ready to appliqué by hand or machine.

## Machine Appliqué

Prepare your background block in the same manner as for hand appliqué. See "Preparing Background Fabric" on page 8.

### Mock Hand Appliqué

This method utilizes the blind hemstitch on your sewing machine. You will need to be able to adjust the length and width of this stitch to use this method successfully. When done well, it is difficult to tell the result from hand appliqué. I used this method to appliqué the center block on "Sweetheart Strawberries" on page 56.

1. Prepare freezer-paper templates and appliqué pieces following steps 1–8 of "Freezer-Paper Appliqué" on page 11.

2. Thread the top of your machine with invisible nylon thread (see "Thread" on page 5). Thread the bobbin with fine thread that matches the background fabric. When threading the bobbin, bring the thread through the "finger" (if your machine has one) on the bobbin to slightly increase bobbin tension. Slightly reduce the top tension as well. Use a fine needle, size 60/8.

3. Use an open-toe embroidery presser foot for this stitch. Set the machine to the blind hemstitch. Shorten the stitch length so that the distance the machine sews straight, between the stitches that swing to the left, is no more than ¼". Adjust the stitch width so that the needle swings to the left no more than ¹⁄₁₆".

4. Make a test piece with fabric scraps to check your stitch. Sew along the edge of a piece of folded fabric so that the straight stitches are in the background fabric and the swing stitch just catches the edge of the folded piece. The bobbin thread should not show on the top. Readjust the machine as necessary to achieve the proper stitch.

Folded test appliqué strip

5. Pin or glue the pieces in place on the background block. Stitch in numerical order. Sew slowly, turning and pivoting the block as needed. Make sure the points are secured by a swing stitch on each side. You can tug the fabric a bit to hold it back so the swing stitch is where you want it to be if necessary. Secure the thread ends by backstitching a few stitches. (The backstitches will not show on the front because of the invisible thread.)

6. When the appliqué is complete, remove the freezer paper and glue, referring to steps 10–12 of "Freezer-Paper Appliqué" on page 12.

### Fusible Appliqué

Quick and easy, this is a great method for seasonal projects and quilts that will not have heavy use. My quilt "Strawberries All Around" on page 20 was done with fusible web and a machine blanket stitch. Be sure to prewash all fabrics used for fusible appliqué.

Before stitching, practice on a sample piece to be sure the stitch is the right size and that the tension is right. You can use thread that matches the appliqué pieces or a contrasting thread. Use an open-toe presser foot so you can see the stitching line clearly.

1. Trace the appliqué pieces onto the paper side of the fusible web. If the pieces are asymmetrical, they must be reversed. (See step 1 of "Template-Free Needle-Turn Appliqué" on page 10 for instructions on tracing a pattern in reverse.) Leave at least ½" of space around each piece to make cutting easier.

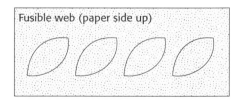

Fusible web (paper side up)

2. Roughly cut the pieces out of the fusible web, leaving at least a ¼" margin all around each piece. For larger pieces, or where pieces will be layered, cut the center of the fusible web away. This will help keep your quilt from being stiff.

3. Follow the manufacturer's instructions to fuse the appliqué shapes to the wrong side of the appliqué fabrics.

4. Cut out the appliqué pieces right on the drawn line. Carefully remove the paper backing.

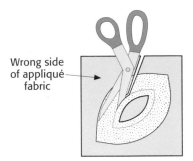

Wrong side of appliqué fabric

5. Place the appliqué pieces on the background fabric. (See "Preparing Background Fabric" on page 8 for placement help.) Fuse the pieces to the background according to the manufacturer's instructions.

6. Stitch around the edges of the appliqué pieces to prevent fraying and to permanently secure them to the background fabric. If your machine has a buttonhole or blanket stitch, this is a good one to use. Stitch so that the straight part of the stitch is on the background fabric, very close to the appliqué edge, and the swing stitch is in the appliqué piece. If you prefer, you can use a narrow zigzag stitch on the edges of the appliqué.

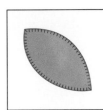 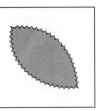

Buttonhole or Blanket Stitch          Zigzag Stitch

# Embroidery

Some of the appliqué patterns in Strawberry Fair include easy embroidered details using these two simple stitches.

## Stem Stitch

The stem stitch is perfect for outlining and adding thin vines and tendrils. Use two or three strands of floss in the needle.

1. Bring the needle up at A; insert it at B. Bring it up again at C, halfway between A and B. Draw the thread through, holding the thread to the right of the needle.

2. Insert the needle at D and bring it up again at B in the same hole the thread went in at B in step 1. Draw the thread through, keeping it to the right of the needle. To finish, knot the thread on the back of the fabric. Weave the thread through the stitches on the wrong side, and then clip the thread.

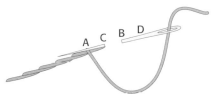

### Marking Embroidery Lines
A fine-point mechanical pencil is easy to use to lightly mark embroidery lines. The fine line is easily covered with your embroidery stitches.

## French Knots

French knots are wonderful, whether used singly for details like bird's eyes or in clusters to make flower centers. Use all six strands of floss in the needle.

1. Bring the needle up at A where you want the knot to be. Wrap the thread around the needle once.

2. Insert the needle into the fabric right next to A and pull the thread until it is snug around the needle. Pull the needle and thread through to the back. There will be a nice tidy knot on the front.

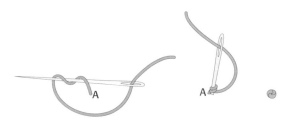

# Borders

Choosing borders for a quilt is much like choosing a frame for a picture. Whenever possible, I like to wait until the center of the quilt is complete before making a final decision on borders. Before you cut your borders, audition the fabric, or combination of fabrics, to find a choice just right for your quilt.

Border measurements are given for projects that include borders, but because variations may crop up during stitching and pressing, always measure your own work before cutting borders.

## Straight-Cut Borders

Straight-cut borders are the simplest to make. The side borders are added first, then the top and bottom borders. When a quilt has inner and outer straight-cut borders, add the inner border to all four sides first, and then add the outer border.

1. Measure the length of the quilt top through its center. Cut side borders of the required width to match this measurement. Use a pin to mark the center of each border strip and the center of each side of the quilt. Pin the borders to the quilt top, matching the center points and outer edges; then stitch. Press the seam allowances toward the borders.

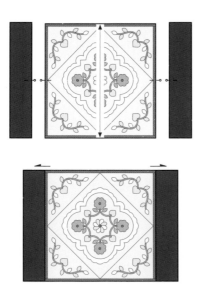

2. Measure the width of the quilt through the center, including the side borders just added. Cut top and bottom borders of the required width to match this measurement. Pin and sew the top and bottom borders to the quilt top as described in step 1. Press the seam allowances toward the borders.

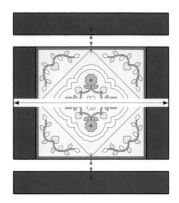

## Mitered Borders

Mitered borders require a little more time and attention than straight-cut borders, but they aren't difficult, and they give a quilt a polished look. They are especially effective when striped fabrics are used.

When the quilt has more than one border to be mitered, cut all the border strips for each side the same length as the outermost border and sew them together so they can be sewn to the quilt and mitered as a single unit.

There are a number of ways to sew mitered borders. Because I also like to appliqué, I sew the miters closed by hand. It's a simple method, and because I work from the right side, it's nearly foolproof, especially for multiple or striped borders.

1. Measure the quilt top through the center as for straight-cut borders. Estimate the final outside measurements of the quilt by adding the widths of all borders, and then add an extra 2". Cut the border strips to this length.

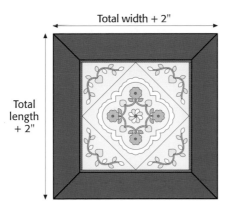

Total width + 2"

Total length + 2"

2. Use pins to mark the center of each border strip and the center of each side of the quilt top. On each border strip, measure and mark one-half the length (or width) of the quilt top from each side of the center pin.

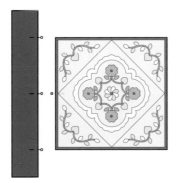

3. Place the border strips and quilt top right sides together, matching the center and the outer pins to the raw edges of the quilt top. Sew the border to the quilt top, beginning and ending with a backstitch ¼" from the corners of the quilt top. Press the seams toward the borders. Repeat on each side of the quilt.

4. To make the miters, lay the quilt on an ironing board so the top border extends over the side borders. Fold under one corner of the top border at a 45° angle. Use a ruler with a 45° line to check that the fold is exactly 45° degrees all the way to

the outer corner. Press the fold firmly and pin it securely, placing pins perpendicular to the fold.

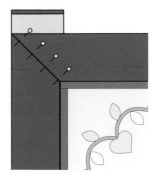

5. Hand sew the miter on the right side with tiny, invisible appliqué stitches. This will be a main construction seam in the quilt; sew it securely. Repeat this process for the remaining three miters. Trim the seams to ¼" and press them open.

# Finishing

You've completed the top, and now it's time for the next stage. First you need to choose a backing and batting. Select backing fabric that complements the front of the quilt and the binding fabric. The backing should be approximately 4" larger than the top, all the way around. Piece the backing together by sewing the seam down the center or in three sections. Press the seams open to minimize bulk.

Your choice of batting may depend on your quilting plan. For machine-quilted quilts, I prefer to use a lightweight to medium-weight cotton batting. The quilt will shrink up just a bit when it is washed and help hide the machine stitching, giving the quilt more of an antique look. For hand quilting I like to use polyester batting because it is much easier for me to needle. Whichever fiber you choose, use a good quality batting; many lovely quilts have been ruined by "bargain batting." Too much time and love go into making the top to compromise on what's inside. Cut the batting approximately 3" larger than the top, all the way around.

## Layering and Basting

Working on a flat surface, place the backing wrong side up, add the batting, and then add the top, smoothing out any wrinkles. Baste through all layers, beginning in the center and working out in each direction, keeping the layers smooth. For hand quilting, baste a line approximately every 4" in each direction in a grid pattern and then all around the outside edge. Many machine quilters prefer to baste with safety pins, layering the "sandwich" in the same way, but using pins to secure the layers.

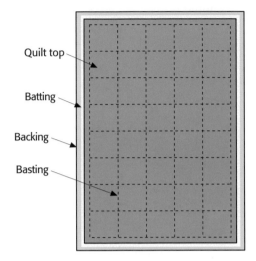

## Quilting

The quilting designs you choose for your quilt will depend on your own preferences and on how you plan to use the quilt. Hand quilting is a lovely way to finish a quilt and is especially nice on an appliquéd quilt that has a plain background to show off your stitching. If you wish to use an elaborate quilting pattern, it is easiest to mark the top before it is layered with the backing and batting. If your quilting plan is simple, like outline or straight-line quilting, you can mark as you go. Don't forget to test your marking tool to be sure the marks can be removed. For hand quilting, most quilters prefer to work with the quilt in a hoop or frame. Begin quilting in the center of the quilt and work out in each direction. Avoid skipping around, which can cause unwanted puckers and bumps.

For machine quilting, straight lines or continuous-line patterns are easiest to do neatly. Use an even-feed, or "walking," foot on your machine so the layers will move through the feed dogs evenly. Set your machine at 8 to 10 stitches per inch. Remove safety pins as you sew.

The two large quilts in this book were machine quilted by a professional using a long-arm quilting machine. They were made for use on beds and may have hard wear, so professional machine quilting was a durable and time-efficient choice. Professional machine quilting is widely available and can be a good way to finish a quilt so you can use and enjoy it sooner.

## Binding

Bias binding is a good choice for quilts likely to be well used. Yardage requirements for bias binding are included with all *Strawberry Fair* projects.

1. Use a rotary cutter and ruler to trim the sides of the quilt so that all layers are even, and the corners are square. Baste the three layers together all around the edge so they won't shift while you apply the binding.

2. Measure the quilt and add the outside dimensions of the quilt (the perimeter); add 9" to this measurement. This is the length of binding you will need for your quilt. Cut the binding strips 2½" wide, on the bias. Join the strips with diagonal seams and press them open.

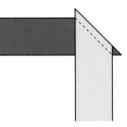

3. Fold the binding in half lengthwise with wrong sides together and press. Fold under a ¼" seam allowance at one end of the long strip.

Fold line

4. Lay the binding on the front of the quilt, aligning all the raw edges. Place the end of the binding several inches from a corner. Begin stitching 4" from the end of the binding. (You want to leave an unsewn tail.) Sew with a ⅜" seam allowance. Stop stitching ⅜" from the corner and backstitch.

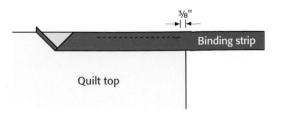

⅜"

Binding strip

Quilt top

**Needle Note**

Use a heavier machine needle to sew the binding to the quilt. I use a size 90/14. To keep the layers from shifting while you stitch, usea walking foot when applying the binding.

5. Fold the binding up at a 45° angle so that it is perpendicular to the edge you just stitched.

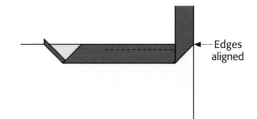

Edges aligned

6. Fold the binding straight down so that the fold is even with the edge of the quilt. Start sewing at the folded edge and then backstitch. Continue stitching around the quilt until you are 4" from the starting point.

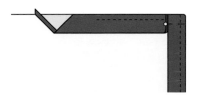

7. Trim the edge of the binding so it overlaps the beginning by 3". Tuck the cut end of the binding strip inside the diagonal fold. Be sure that the join is smooth on the long folded edge. Pin, and then finish sewing the binding to the quilt.

8. Fold the binding over the edge of the quilt and hand stitch it to the backing, using the appliqué stitch. As you fold each corner back, a miter will form on the front. To make a similar miter on the back, fold down one side of the binding, and then the other. Finish the binding by hand, stitching the diagonal folds of the miters and the diagonal seam where the binding ends.

## Labeling

If only our quilting ancestors had labeled their quilts, we would know so much more about the quilts and about our ancestors' lives. One day your great-granddaughters and great-great-granddaughters may want to know more about you and your quilts. Making a label for your quilt is a gift you can give future generations. Your label should include your name, the date you completed the quilt, and where it was made. If you made the quilt for a special occasion or as a gift, include that information as well.

**Quilt Care**

You might also want to add information on the quilt label to let the lucky recipient know how to care for the quilt.

## Hanging Sleeve

If you plan to hang your quilt, make a hanging sleeve and attach it to the back of the quilt. The sleeve will help the quilt to hang properly and will evenly distribute the weight of the quilt.

1. Measure the width of the quilt and cut a strip of fabric 8½" wide by the measurement of the quilt. Use the backing fabric, if you have enough left over, so that the sleeve will blend in with the quilt.

2. Fold the strip in half lengthwise, right sides together, and sew a ¼" seam along the long edge. Press the seam open.

3. Fold the short ends back ¼" and then 1" to make a hem. Stitch the hem on each side by hand or machine.

4. Turn the sleeve right side out and press so that the seam is centered on the side of the sleeve that will face the back of the quilt.

5. Hand sew the top and bottom edges of the sleeve to the top edge of the quilt back, just below the binding. Take care to sew only through the quilt backing; do not stitch through to the front of the quilt.

# Strawberries All Around

Made by Elizabeth Hamby Carlson, 2004; quilted by Sheri Flemming.

Finished quilt: 62" x 62" ● Finished block: 10" x 10"

*The inspiration* for this quilt design began with one fabric—the beautiful pink and blue floral I found while vacationing in Colorado. I knew immediately that the airy floral design in the fabric would complement appliquéd strawberry blocks to create a charming and feminine quilt. Fusible appliqué, combined with a machine buttonhole stitch, made the strawberry blocks a snap to make. The quick-and-easy pieced alternate blocks add a lovely secondary pattern. Gather together some fabrics that you love, and in no time at all you can stitch up a strawberry patch of your own.

# Materials

3 yards of large-scale floral print for setting blocks, outer border, and binding

1⅛ yards of light fabric for appliqué background

1 yard of small-scale floral print for setting blocks and border corner squares

⅞ yard of light blue fabric for sashing and inner border

½ yard of dark green for middle circles and leaves

⅜ yard of medium green for leaves

⅜ yard of light green for large circles

⅜ yard of dark pink for berries and sashing squares

¼ yard of red for berries

⅛ yard of green plaid for small circles

4 yards of fabric for backing

68" x 68" piece of batting

Fusible web (optional)

# Cutting

## Appliqué Blocks *(see pattern on page 25)*

**From the light background fabric, cut:**

9 squares, 11½" x 11½"

**From the light green fabric, cut:**

9 of circle #1

**From the dark green fabric, cut:**

9 of circle #2

36 of leaf #5

36 of leaf #6

**From the green plaid, cut:**

9 of circle #3

**From the red fabric, cut:**

36 of berry #4

**From the dark pink fabric, cut:**

36 of berry #4

**From the medium green fabric, cut:**

36 of leaf #5

36 of leaf #6

## Setting Blocks and Triangles

**From the large-scale floral print, cut:**

2 squares, 11¼" x 11¼"

4 squares, 9½" x 9½"

**From the small-scale floral print, cut:**

2 squares, 11¼" x 11¼"

6 squares, 9½" x 9½"; cut 2 squares once diagonally to make 4 triangles

### Sashing and Borders

**From the light blue fabric, cut:**

36 strips, 1½" x 10½"

7 strips, 1½" x 40"

**From the dark pink fabric, cut:**

28 squares, 1½" x 1½"

**From the large-scale floral print, cut:**

4 strips, 6½" x 50½"

**From the small-scale floral print, cut:**

4 squares, 6½" x 6½"

# Appliqué Blocks

Appliqué the strawberry blocks following the steps below for fusible appliqué, or use the appliqué method of your choice.

1. Fold the 11½" background squares into quarters diagonally and press lightly to mark the appliqué placement lines.

2. Referring to "Fusible Appliqué" on page 14, use the appliqué pattern on page 25 to prepare and cut out appliqué pieces. Follow the manufacturer's instructions for the fusible web.

3. Arrange the appliqué pieces on the blocks in numerical order, using the pressed lines and the pattern as a guide to placement. Fuse, following the manufacturer's instructions.

4. Using a buttonhole stitch, machine stitch around the edges of the appliqués. I chose thread colors to match the appliqués. For a different look, you could use black thread for all the buttonhole stitching.

5. Trim and square up the appliqué blocks to measure 10½", referring to "Squaring Up Blocks" on page 7.

# Making the Setting Blocks and Triangles

1. Layer an 11¼" large-scale floral square and an 11¼" small-scale floral square right sides together. Draw two diagonal lines on the wrong side of the lighter fabric from corner to corner.

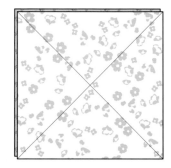

2. Sew a ¼" seam on each side of one of the diagonal lines. Cut on the drawn line between the stitched lines. Press the seams toward the darker fabric.

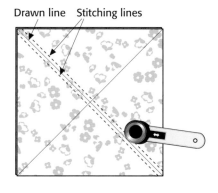

Drawn line    Stitching lines

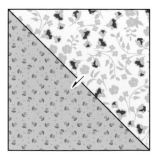

3. Layer the new squares right sides together so the contrasting fabrics face each other and the seam allowances oppose each other. Extend the drawn line to the corner. Sew a ¼" seam on both sides of the diagonal line. Cut on the marked line between the stitching. Press each new unit open; you will have two hourglass setting blocks.

Drawn line   Stitching lines

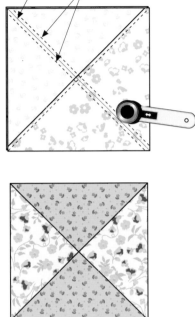

4. Repeat steps 1 through 3 to make two more hour-glass blocks.

5. Make two Four Patch blocks, as shown, using the 9½" x 9½" large- and small-scale floral squares.

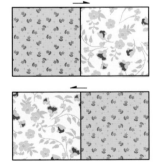 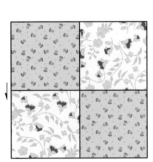

Make 2.

6. Cut each Four Patch block twice diagonally to yield four side setting triangles for a total of eight.

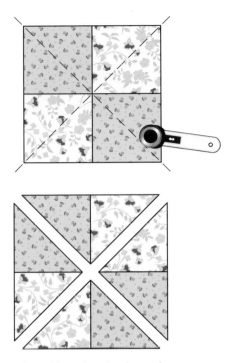

Make 8 side setting triangles total.

## Assembling the Quilt

1. Arrange the appliqué blocks, hourglass blocks, and setting triangles with the sashing strips and sashing squares in diagonal rows as shown. Sew each row together and press all the seam allowances toward the blue sashing strips. Join the rows and

press all the seam allowances toward the sashing strips to complete the center of the quilt.

2. Sew the 1½" x 40" inner-border strips end to end to make one continuous 1½"-wide inner-border strip. Referring to "Straight-Cut Borders" on page 16 as needed, measure the quilt and cut four inner-border strips all the same length. Sew two of these strips to opposite sides of the quilt. Press the seam allowances toward the border strips.

3. Sew a 1½" pink square to each end of the remaining two inner-border strips. Press the seam allowances toward the blue inner-border strips.

4. Sew inner-border strips to the top and bottom of the quilt. Press the seam allowances toward the blue inner border.

5. Pin and sew two 6½"-wide outer-border strips to opposite sides of the quilt. Press the seam allowances toward the inner borders.

6. Sew a 6½" small-scale floral square to each end of the remaining two outer-border strips. Press the seam allowances toward the squares.

7. Sew the outer borders to the top and bottom of the quilt. Press the seam allowances toward the inner border.

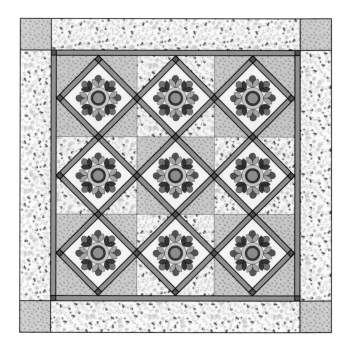

# Finishing the Quilt

Refer to "Finishing" on page 17 for detailed instructions if needed.

1. Piece the quilt backing. Center the quilt top and batting over the backing and baste through all layers.

2. Quilt as desired, by hand or machine.

3. Trim the excess backing and batting. Cut the binding fabric into 2½"-wide bias strips. Sew the binding to the quilt.

4. Make a hanging sleeve and sew it to your quilt, if you wish, and label your quilt.

**Appliqué Patterns
and Placement Guide**

4

6

5

1

2

3

Center

# Pineapple and Strawberry Table Runner

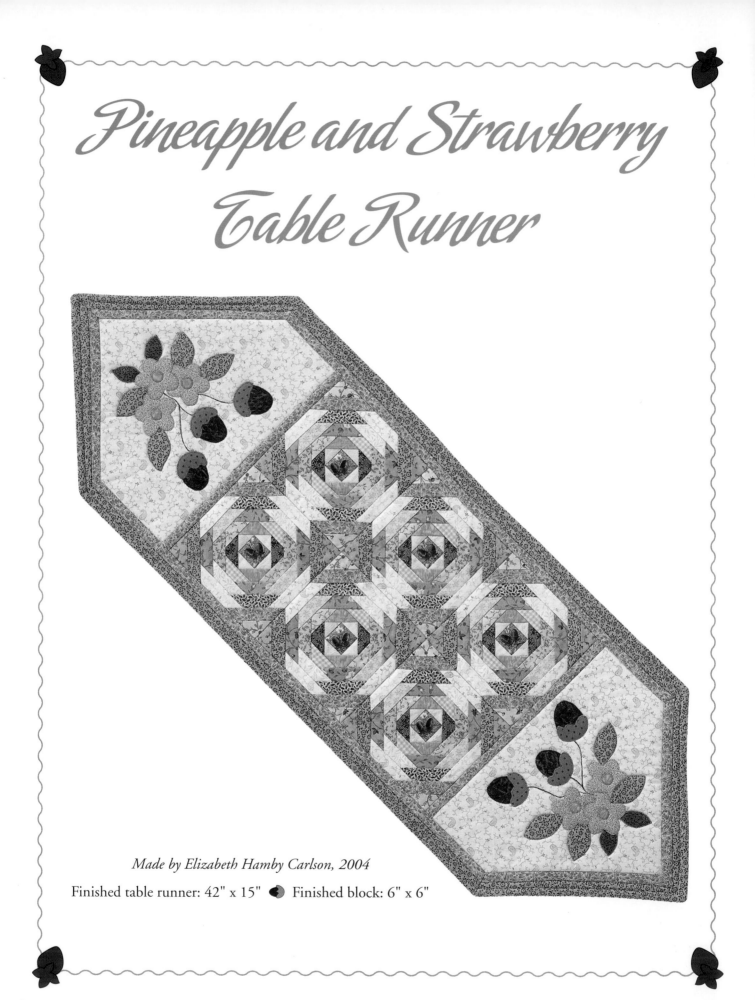

*Made by Elizabeth Hamby Carlson, 2004*

Finished table runner: 42" x 15"    Finished block: 6" x 6"

*Welcome spring* with a pretty table runner pieced with lots of pastel fabrics and finished off with cheerful appliquéd berries and blossoms. I chose colors to coordinate with the pink and green dishes my family likes to use for Easter dinner. The Pineapple blocks in the center are easily and accurately foundation pieced—the perfect method for making these blocks. If you haven't tried it before, here's a good opportunity. You (and your friends and family) will be impressed with the accuracy you'll achieve! Fusible appliqué makes the strawberries quick and easy too, but you can use your favorite method of appliqué.

# Materials

⅜ yard of green print for outer border and blocks

¼ yard of gold print for inner border and blocks

¼ yard *each* of at least four assorted light fabrics for Pineapple blocks

¼ yard *each* of at least five assorted dark fabrics for Pineapple blocks

1 fat quarter of light fabric for appliqué background

Scraps of red, green, blue, and gold for appliqué

1¼ yards of fabric for backing

19" x 46" piece of lightweight batting

# Cutting

## Pineapple Blocks

**From the assorted light fabrics, cut a *total* of:**

9 strips, 1¼" x 40"

12 squares, 1¾" x 1¾", cut once diagonally to make 24 triangles

**From the assorted dark fabrics, cut a *total* of:**

9 strips, 1¼" x 40"

6 squares, 1¾" x 1¾", for center squares

24 squares, 2¼" x 2¼", cut once diagonally to make 48 triangles

## Appliqué

**From the light background fabric, cut:**

1 square, 15" x 15", cut once diagonally to make 2 triangles

## Borders

**From the gold print, cut:**

2 strips, 1" x 12½"

2 strips, 1" x 32"

4 strips, 1" x 14"

**From the green print, cut:**

2 strips, 1½" x 32"

4 strips, 1½" x 14"

# Piecing the Pineapple Blocks

1. Make six copies of the pineapple foundation pattern on page 32. Use tracing paper or transparent paper specially made for foundation piecing to make your foundations. Being able to see through the paper makes the piecing go more smoothly.

### Easy Foundations

Trace the foundation pattern onto one sheet of tracing paper or other foundation paper, and then stack and staple several sheets of paper together with the traced copy on top. Use your sewing machine without any thread in it to "sew" on the lines to mark the pattern with needlepunched holes.

2. Pin a 1¾" dark square right side up on the center of the unmarked side of the paper foundation. Hold the foundation up to the light so you know that the fabric completely covers the center square on the paper.

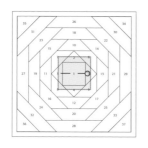

3. Place a 1¾" light triangle on top of the center square, right sides together.

4. Holding the layers in place, turn the square paper side up and position under the presser foot. Stitch on the line between pieces 1 and 2, extending the stitching ¼" beyond the line at the beginning and the end.

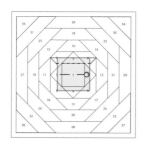

5. Remove from the sewing machine and press the piece to one side with a dry iron.

6. Repeat steps 2–5 to add pieces 3, 4, and 5, using three additional light triangles.

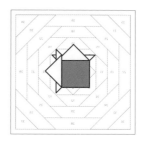

7. Repeat steps 2–6 to add pieces 6, 7, 8, and 9, using dark triangles.

8. Follow the diagram for color placement of light and dark fabrics. Using the 1¼" strips of light and dark fabrics, cut the pieces to the proper length as you go. Continue adding pieces 10 through 33 to the block in numerical order.

9. Using the remaining dark triangles, add corner pieces 34 through 37 to complete the block.

Color Placement
Diagram

10. Trim the block along the outside cutting line.

11. Repeat steps 2–10 to make five more Pineapple blocks. Remove the paper from all of the blocks.

12. Sew the six blocks together as shown.

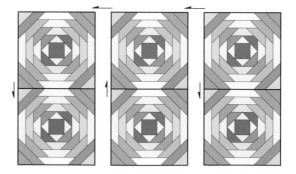

# Appliqué

The appliqué may be done by hand or machine using the method you prefer, referring to "Appliqué" on page 8 as needed. Prepare the appliqué pieces from the red, green, blue, and gold scraps using the pattern on page 33.

1. Fold each background triangle in half and lightly press to mark the centerline.

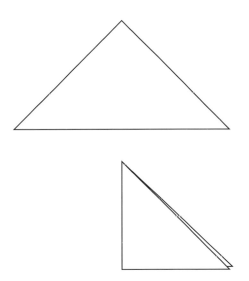

2. Fold the point of the triangle down to meet the long edge and lightly crease to mark the center point of the triangle.

3. Matching centers for accurate placement, use the appliqué pattern on page 33 to appliqué the pieces onto each triangle. Follow the numerical order on the pattern.

4. Use either a permanent-ink pen or embroidery floss (see "Embroidery" on page 15) to add stems to the strawberries.

# Assembling the Table Runner

1. Sew a 1" x 12½" gold strip to each end of the Pineapple block section. Press the seam allowances toward the gold.

2. Center an appliqué triangle section on each end of the center section and sew to the gold border strip. Press the seam allowances toward the gold. Trim the excess triangle fabric away so that the sides of the triangles are even with the center section.

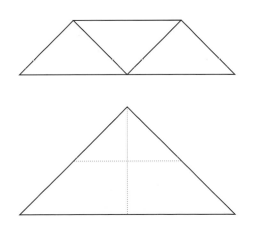

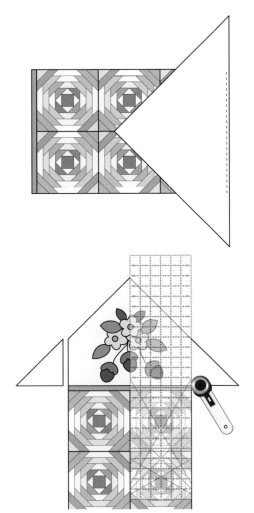

3. Sew the borders together by joining the green and gold strips of corresponding table lengths as shown.

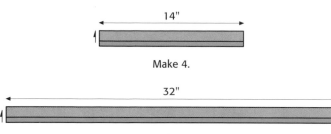

14"

Make 4.

32"

Make 2.

4. Sew two 14"-long border strips to each end of the table runner as shown. Begin and end your stitching ¼" from the raw edge of the appliqué triangle. Press the seam allowances toward the border.

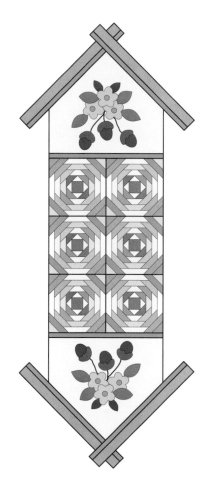

5. Referring to "Mitered Borders" on page 16 as needed, miter the borders at the ends of the table runner.

6. Center a 32"-long border strip on one long edge of the table runner. Sew, beginning and ending the stitching ¼" from the raw edge of the table runner. Press the seam allowances toward the gold.

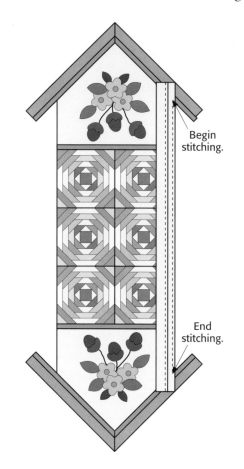

Begin stitching.

End stitching.

7. Fold an end of the 32"-long border strip back so that the fold meets the 14"-long border strip in a shallow miter. Press the fold. Hand sew the fold to the 14" border strip to close the miter in the same manner as for a 45° miter. Trim the excess fabric. Repeat for the other end of the 32"-long border strip.

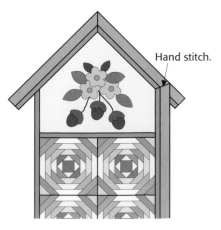

Hand stitch.

8. Repeat steps 6 and 7 to add the remaining border strip to the other side.

sides together. Sew a ¼" seam all around the table runner, leaving a 9" opening on one long side for turning.

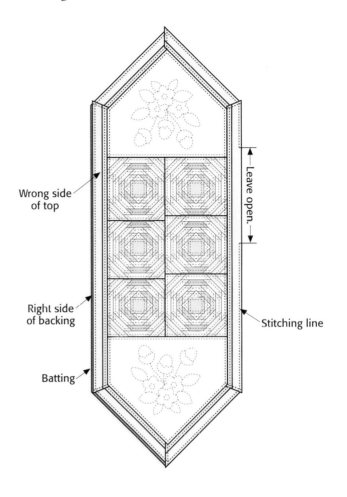

Wrong side
of top

Right side
of backing

Batting

Leave open

Stitching line

# Finishing the Table Runner

1. Cut a piece of backing fabric and batting the same size as the table runner.

2. Layer the batting, backing, and table runner, with the backing fabric and the completed top right

3. Turn the table runner right side out and press. Fold in the edges of the 9" opening and sew closed by hand.

4. Quilt as desired, by hand or machine.

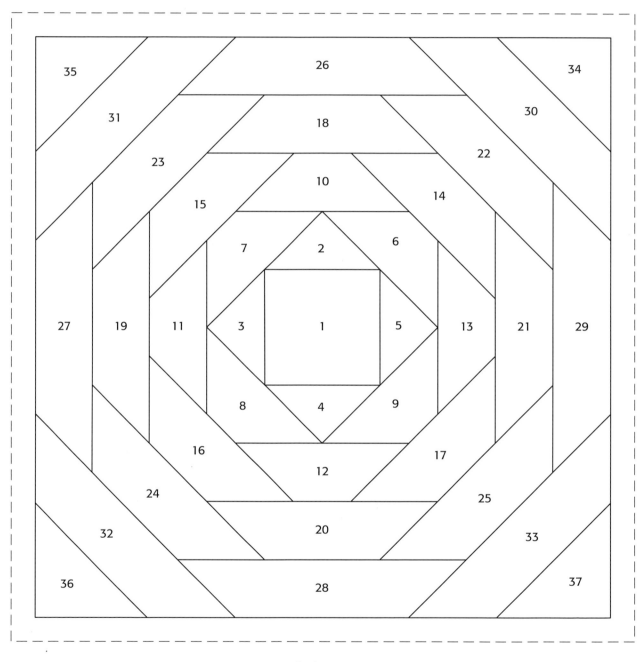

**Foundation Pattern**

## Appliqué Patterns and Placement Guide

"Pineapple and Strawberry Table Runner" – Green
"Sweetheart Strawberries" Quilt – Red

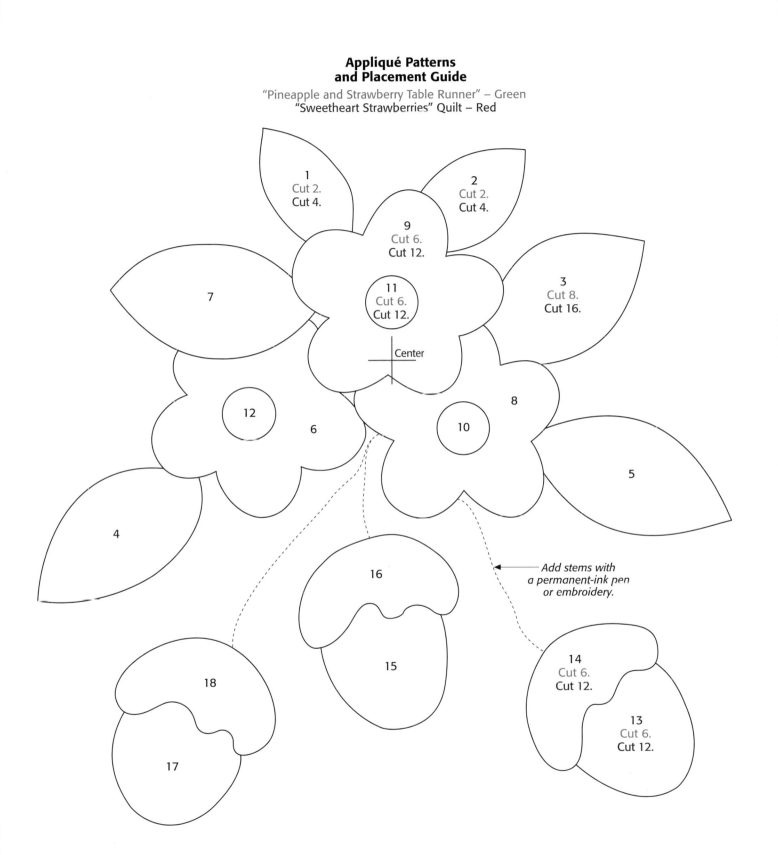

1
Cut 2.
Cut 4.

2
Cut 2.
Cut 4.

9
Cut 6.
Cut 12.

11
Cut 6.
Cut 12.

3
Cut 8.
Cut 16.

7

Center

12

6

8

10

4

5

16

15

Add stems with
a permanent-ink pen
or embroidery.

14
Cut 6.
Cut 12.

18

17

13
Cut 6.
Cut 12.

# Strawberry Fair Album

*Made by Elizabeth Hamby Carlson, 2003*

Finished quilt: 48¼" x 48¼" ● Finished block: 10" x 10"

*Nine gorgeous blocks*—including strawberry wreaths, birds, and sprays of strawberries—surround a central basket of strawberries and blossoms in a classic nineteenth-century American-style album quilt. Each block is embellished with embroidery details and framed with a narrow green border and floral print sashing. Simple borders finish the quilt, allowing the appliqué designs to take center stage. Hand quilting adds the crowning touch to a special quilt. Choose your favorite appliqué technique and enjoy stitching a strawberry album quilt to treasure for years to come.

# Materials

2½ yards of green print for appliqués, block frames, outer border, and binding

1⅝ yards of floral print for sashing

1⅛ yards of light fabric for appliqué background

⅜ yard of dark pink print for inner border

Scraps of assorted pinks, reds, greens, blues, and golds for appliqués

3⅛ yards of fabric for backing

54" x 54" piece of batting

Brown and gold embroidery floss

# Cutting

## Blocks

**From the light background fabric, cut:**

9 squares, 11½" x 11½"

**From the green print, cut:**

18 strips, 1⅛" x 10½"

18 strips, 1⅛" x 11¾"

## Sashing and Borders

**From the floral print, cut:**

6 strips, 2" x 11¾"

2 strips, 2" x 37¼"

4 strips, 2" x 50"

**From the dark pink print, cut:**

5 strips, 1¼" x 40"

**From the green print, cut:**

4 strips, 4" x 50"

# Appliqué Blocks

I chose to hand appliqué my quilt using the template-free needle-turn method described on page 10, which I find very relaxing. Appliqué your album quilt using the hand or machine appliqué method you prefer. Refer to "Appliqué" on page 8.

1. Fold each 11½" background square in quarters to find the center, and then crease each square diagonally to help place the appliqués accurately. Using the block patterns on pages 38–49, mark block designs on the background as appropriate for your appliqué method.

2. The appliqué order is marked on each block pattern in alphabetical and numerical order. Appliqué the stems first, in alphabetical order, and then appliqué the rest of the pieces in numerical order.

## Appliqué Tip

For the center basket block, appliqué the diagonal strips on the basket fabric before you cut out and appliqué the basket itself. That way you can tuck the raw ends of the diagonal strips under the bottom and side edges of the basket.

3. Add embroidery to the blocks where indicated on the block designs, referring to "Embroidery" on page 15.

4. Carefully and gently press the completed appliqué blocks and trim to measure 10½" x 10½". See "Squaring Up Blocks" on page 7.

5. Sew two 1⅛" x 10½" green framing strips to opposite sides of each block. Press seam allowances toward the green strips. Sew a 1⅛" x 11¾" green framing strip to the top and bottom of each block. Press seam allowances toward the green strips.

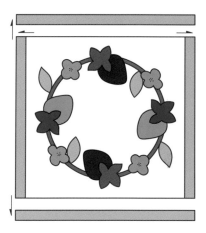

# Assembling the Quilt

1. Arrange the appliqué blocks and the 2" x 11¾" and 2" x 37¼" floral print sashing strips as shown. Sew the blocks and horizontal sashing strips into vertical rows. Press all the seam allowances toward the blocks. Add the vertical sashing strips to complete the center of the quilt. Press.

2. Join the five pink 1¼" inner-border strips end to end to make one continuous strip. From this, cut four inner-border strips, 50" long.

3. Make a border unit by sewing together one 2"-wide floral strip, one dark pink inner-border strip, and one green print outer-border strip. Press the seam allowances toward the pink inner border. Make four border units.

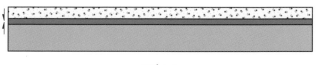

Make 4.

4. Referring to "Mitered Borders" on page 16, measure, pin, and sew the borders to the quilt. Press the seam allowances toward the center of the quilt. Miter the corners. Press.

# Finishing the Quilt

Refer to "Finishing" on page 17 for detailed instructions if needed.

1. Piece the quilt backing. Center the quilt top and batting over the backing, and baste through all layers.

2. Quilt as desired, by hand or machine.

3. Trim the excess backing and batting. Cut the binding fabric into 2½"-wide bias strips. Sew the binding to the quilt.

4. Make a hanging sleeve and sew it to your quilt, if you wish, and label your quilt.

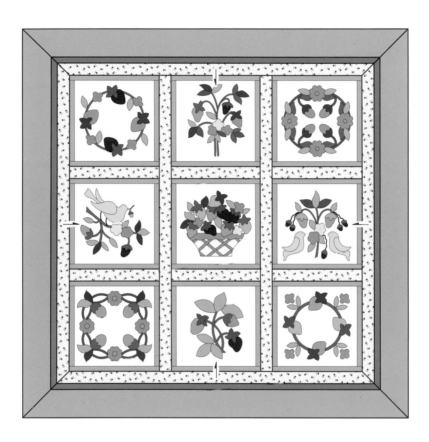

**Appliqué Patterns and Placement Guide**

French knots

4

D

6

3

7

C

Center

1

2

B

8

5

A

+

**Appliqué Patterns**

Center

French knots

**Appliqué Patterns**

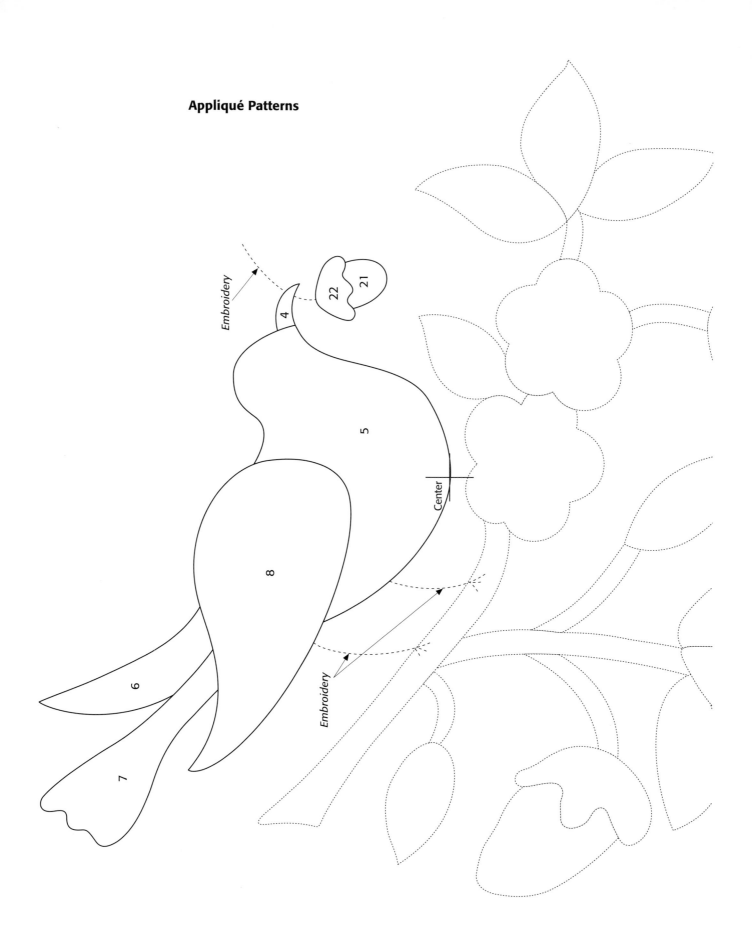

Center

**Appliqué Patterns**

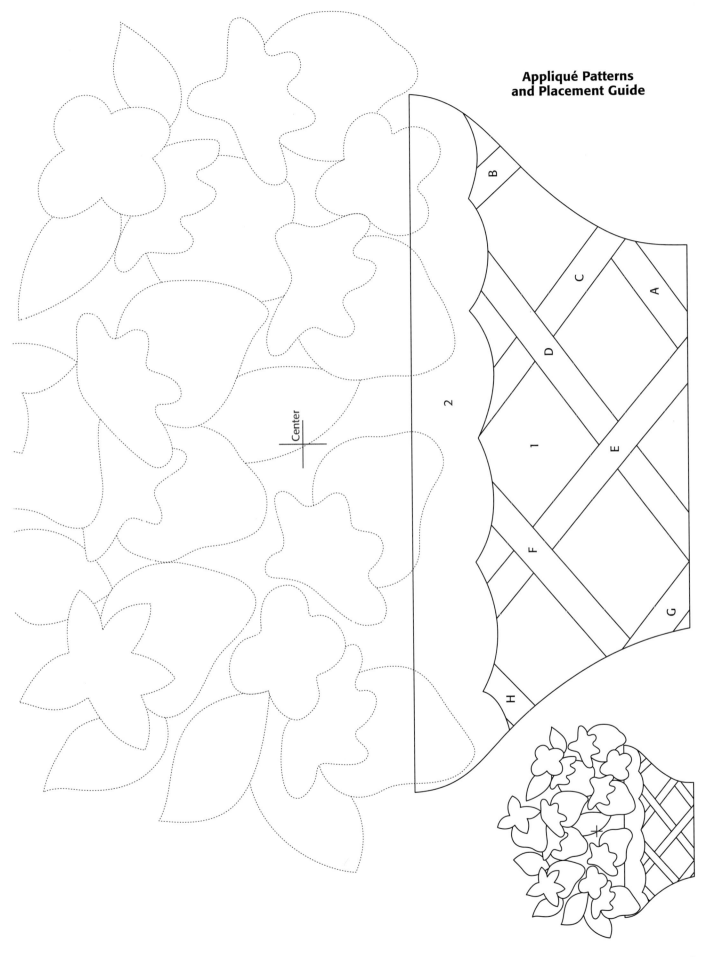

**Appliqué Patterns
and Placement Guide**

Center

2

B

C

A

D

1

E

F

G

H

**Appliqué Patterns and Placement Guide**

15

14

13

18

8

B

D

C

Embroidery

17

7

22

21

16

3

Center

6

20

5

French knots

19

2

French knots

1

French knots

24

23

4

Embroidery

A

28

27

**Appliqué Patterns**

Center

Embroidery

12

11

10

9

French knot

25

26

**Appliqué Patterns
and Placement Guide**

Center

**Appliqué Patterns**

Appliqué Patterns
and Placement Guide

7

6

5

A

2

1

4

3

B

9

8

10

French knots

**Appliqué Patterns and Placement Guide**

8

11

10

12

7

9

A

C

D

1

2

14

16

(A)

13

15

5

6

Center

(B)

4

3

B

# Strawberries in the Garden

*Made by Elizabeth Hamby Carlson, 2004; quilted by Sheri Flemming.*

Finished quilt: 83" x 96"

*Most quilters know* what it is like to fall in love with a prima donna fabric, a fabric so beautiful it needs to be showcased, not cut in pieces too small to appreciate. The main fabric in this quilt, covered with strawberries and roses, is one of those fabrics. As soon as I spotted it on the shelf in the quilt shop, I began to plan a quilt that would let the fabric be the "star of the show." The plain blocks are set in the traditional Garden Maze. The sashing and corner squares go together so quickly that you can have a big bed quilt done in record time. Gorgeous fabric and nearly instant gratification—a perfect combination!

# Materials

4⅛ yards of medium green fabric for sashing strips, sashing corner squares, and binding

3⅝ yards of large-scale floral fabric for blocks and borders*

2⅝ yards of small-scale floral fabric for sashing strips and sashing corner squares

⅜ yard of dark green fabric for sashing corner squares

9 yards of fabric for backing

89" x 102" piece of batting

*If you wish to "fussy cut" the large-scale print you will need to increase this yardage, taking into account the size of the pattern repeat in your fabric.*

# Cutting

**From the medium green fabric, cut:**

38 strips, 1¾" x 40"

108 squares, 4⅝" x 4⅝"

**From the small-scale floral fabric, cut:**

19 strips, 3" x 40"

52 squares, 3¾" x 3¾"; cut squares twice diagonally to make 208 template B triangles

4 squares, 4⅝" x 4⅝"; cut squares once diagonally to make 8 template D triangles

**From the dark green fabric, cut:**

56 squares, 2¼" x 2¼" (template C)

**From the large-scale floral fabric, cut:**

20 squares, 8½" x 8½"

2 strips, 8½" x 70½"

2 strips, 8½" x 73½"

# Sashing Strips and Squares

1. Make 19 strip sets, 40" long, using two 1¾" x 40" medium green strips and one 3" x 40" small-scale floral strip for each set. Press seam allowances toward the green strips.

Make 19 strip sets.

2. Crosscut the strip sets into 75 segments, 8½" long, for the sashing strips.

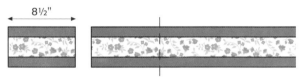

Cut 75 segments.

3. Rotary cut each 4⅝" x 4⅝" medium green square into two prism shapes as shown. Place the 1⅛" line of the ruler on the diagonal line of the green square. Make the cut. Turn the piece and make a second cut, parallel to the first cut, 2¼" away to make a double-pointed prism shape. Measure 3¼" from one of the points and cut the shape into two pieces. Check the accuracy of the pieces against template A on page 55.

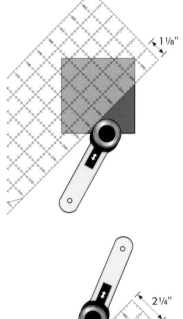

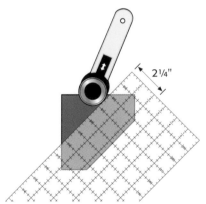

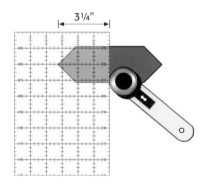

4. Sew two small-scale floral triangle B pieces to opposite sides of a prism A. Press the seam allowances toward prism A. Make 104 of this unit. Check the accuracy of the unit against template D on page 55.

Make 104.

5. Sew two prism A pieces to opposite sides of each dark green 2¼" square C. Press the seam allowances toward prism A. Make 56.

Make 56.

6. Assemble the sashing square units as shown. Press the seam allowances toward the center of the block. Make 48 sashing squares.

Make 48.

7. Make eight corner sashing blocks using the remaining eight prism-triangle units from step 4, eight prism-and-square units from step 5, and eight D triangles.

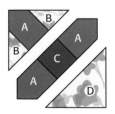

Make 8.

# Assembling the Quilt

1. Arrange the 8½" squares, 49 of the sashing strips, 26 of the sashing squares, and four of the sashing corner blocks in rows as shown in the assembly diagram. Sew each row together, pressing the seam allowances toward the sashing.

2. Join the rows to make the quilt center, pressing the seam allowances toward the sashing rows.

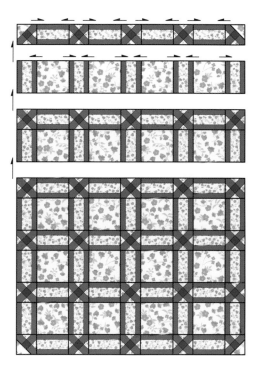

3. Sew the two 8½" x 70½" large-scale floral inner-border strips to opposite sides of the quilt. Press the seam allowances toward the center of quilt.

Add the 8½" x 73½" inner-border strips to the top and bottom of the quilt. Press the seam allowances toward the center of the quilt.

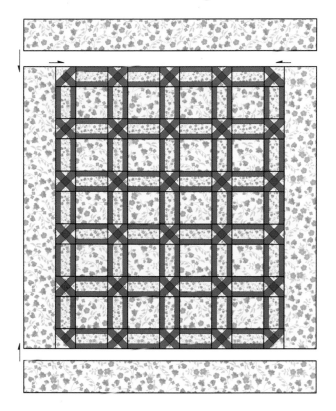

### Pressing Advice

I pressed the seams toward the pieced border to give the narrow dark green strips a little more dimension in the finished quilt. You can press whichever way you prefer.

4. Make two side outer-border strips by joining seven sashing strips and six sashing squares. Press the seam allowances toward the sashing strips. Sew to opposite sides of the quilt and press toward the inner border.

5. Make the top and bottom outer borders by joining six sashing strips, five sashing squares, and two
sashing corner squares. Press the seam allowances
toward the sashing strips. Sew to the top and bottom of the quilt. Press.

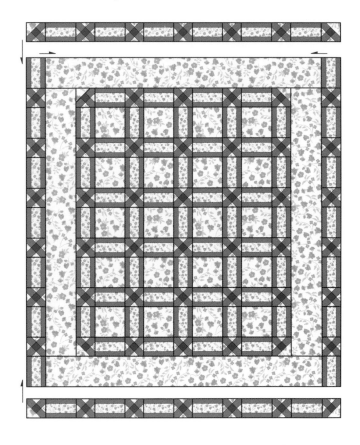

# Finishing the Quilt

Refer to "Finishing" on page 17 for detailed instructions if needed.

1. Piece the quilt backing. Center the quilt top and
   batting over the backing, and baste through all
   layers.

2. Quilt as desired, by hand or machine.

3. Trim the excess backing and batting. Cut the
   binding fabric into 2½"-wide bias strips. Sew the
   binding to the quilt and add a label.

**Template Patterns**

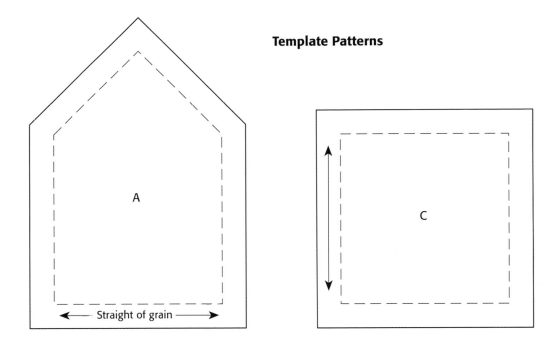

A

Straight of grain

C

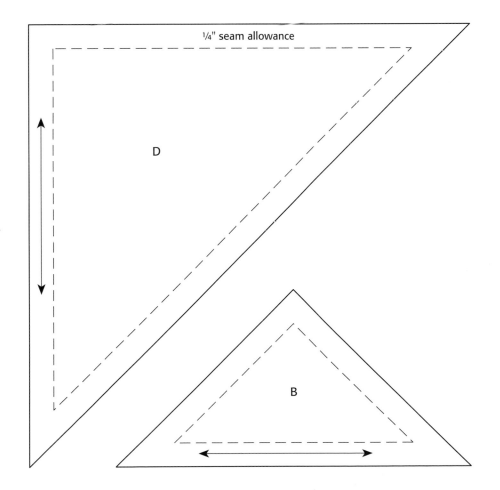

¼" seam allowance

D

B

# Sweetheart Strawberries

*Made by Elizabeth Hamby Carlson, 2004*

Finished quilt: 43" x 43"

*A 200-year-old* English pearlware saucer provided the inspiration for "Sweetheart Strawberries." I'm very fond of antique dishes as well as strawberry patterns, so I'm naturally drawn to crockery decorated with berries. The strawberry wreath on this little saucer spoke to me. I brought it home and immediately began adapting the wreath design for the center block of this quilt. The colors in the quilt are closely drawn from the strong, bright, hand-painted colors of the saucer. The quilt and the colors were a joy to work with. I made this quilt in the winter, and the colors reminded me that spring really was right around the corner.

# Materials

2 yards of dark pink fabric for borders #1, #2, #4, and #5, and binding

1¼ yards of tan print for borders #2, #3, and #4

⅝ yard of light fabric for center appliqué background

⅜ yard of medium pink fabric for borders #2 and #5

Scraps of assorted pinks, reds, and greens for appliqués

2⅞ yards of fabric for backing

49" x 49" piece of batting

# Cutting

## Appliqué Block

**From the light background fabric, cut:**

1 square, 19½" x 19½"

## Borders

**From the dark pink fabric, cut on the lengthwise grain:**

2 strips for border #1, 1½" x 18½"

2 strips for border #1, 1½" x 20½"

2 strips for border #5, 2" x 40½"

2 strips for border #5, 2" x 43½"

24 squares, 3⅜" x 3⅜"

**From the tan print, cut:**

4 strips for border #3, 5½" x 37½"

46 squares, 3⅜" x 3⅜"

4 squares, 3" x 3"

**From the medium pink fabric, cut:**

22 squares, 3⅜" x 3⅜"

# Appliqué Center Block

The center block of the quilt was machine appliquéd. The appliqué pieces were prepared with freezer paper and glue, and then stitched to the background with a mock hand-appliqué stitch. (See "Freezer-Paper Appliqué" on page 11 and "Mock Hand Appliqué" on page 14.) The border appliqués were hand stitched using the template-free needle-turn appliqué method described on page 10. Appliqué your quilt using the appliqué method(s) of your choice.

1. Fold the background square into quarters to find the centerlines, and then crease the block diagonally to help place the appliqués accurately. Referring to "Preparing Background Fabric" on page 8, mark the appliqué patterns on pages 60–63 onto the background fabric as appropriate for your appliqué method.

2. The appliqué order is marked on the pattern in alphabetical and numerical order. Appliqué the stems first, in alphabetical order, and then appliqué the remaining pieces in numerical order.

3. Use a permanent-ink pen to add the very fine strawberry stems, or embroider them with a stem stitch referring to "Embroidery" on page 15.

4. Press the completed appliqué block and trim it to measure 18½" x 18½". See "Squaring Up Blocks" on page 7.

# Border One

1. Sew two 1½" x 18½" border #1 strips to opposite sides of the center block. Press the seam allowances toward the border strips.

2. Sew the 1½" x 20½" border #1 strips to the top and bottom of the center block. Press seam allowances toward the border.

# Border Two

1. Use a pencil to draw a diagonal line, corner to corner, on the wrong side of each 3⅜" tan square.

2. Layer a tan square with a medium pink square, right sides together. On both sides of the drawn line, sew a ¼" seam.

Drawn line    Stitching lines

3. Cut apart diagonally right on the drawn line. You will have two half-square-triangle units. Press the seam allowances toward the pink triangles.

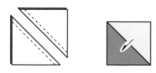

4. Repeat steps 2 and 3 with the 3⅜" dark pink and the remaining 3⅜" tan squares and medium pink

squares. Make 44 tan/medium pink half-square-triangle units and 48 tan/dark pink units. This will be enough for borders #2 and #4.

Make 44.      Make 48.

5. Make border #2 strips by sewing together eight half-square-triangle units, alternating medium pink and dark pink units as shown. Make four.

Make 4.

6. Sew two border #2 strips to opposite sides of the quilt center. Press the seam allowances toward border #1.

7. Add a tan 3" x 3" square to each end of the remaining two border #2 strips. Sew the borders to the top and bottom of the quilt as shown. Press.

# Border Three

Refer to "Mitered Borders" on page 16 as needed. Sew a tan 5½" x 37½" border #3 strip to each side of the quilt. Miter the corners.

# Border Four

Repeat steps 5 and 6 of "Border Two," using 14 half-square-triangle units for each border strip. Repeat step 7, using tan/dark pink half-square-triangle units in place of the plain tan corner squares.

# Border Five

1. Sew the 2" x 40½" border #5 strips to opposite sides of the quilt. Press the seam allowances toward border #5.

2. Sew the 2" x 43½" border #5 strips to the top and bottom of the quilt. Press the seam allowances toward border #5.

# Corner Appliqué

Use the appliqué pattern from the "Pineapple and Strawberry Table Runner" on page 33 to prepare the shapes and appliqué each corner of the quilt. Appliqué the pieces in numerical order as indicated on the pattern. Add strawberry stems with a permanent-ink pen or embroidered stem stitch. See "Embroidery" on page 15.

# Finishing the Quilt

Refer to "Finishing" on page 17 for detailed instructions if needed.

1. Piece the quilt backing. Center the quilt top and batting over the backing, and baste through all layers.

2. Quilt as desired, by hand or machine.

3. Trim the excess backing and batting. Cut the binding fabric into 2½"-wide bias strips. Sew the binding to the quilt.

4. Make a hanging sleeve and sew it to your quilt, if you wish, and label your quilt.

**Appliqué Patterns
and Placement Guide**

Center

Embroidery

G

18
20
21
22
23
24
25
26
27
28
29
30
31
32
33
34
35

**Appliqué Patterns
and Placement Guide**

42

43

48

H

J

39

I

46

45

47

44

41

40

36

37

38

32

34

35

30

33

31

Center

*Sweetheart Strawberries* 🍓 61

**Appliqué Patterns and Placement Guide**

23

G

*Embroidery*

22

18

20

21

19

F

Center

1

16

15

14

13

17

D

C

12

11

E

10

9

**Appliqué Patterns and Placement Guide**

Center

44
47
46
45
H
J
48

1
2
51
50
49

B

A
E
5
6
7
8
4
9

# English Floral Sampler

*Made by Elizabeth Hamby Carlson, 1999*

Finished quilt: 12½" x 24½"

*Young girls* in seventeenth-century England practiced their needlework skills by embroidering "band samplers," long linen panels featuring horizontal rows of floral and geometric motifs. Some years ago, I attended a needlework conference at Colonial Williamsburg where we studied early band samplers. I found the intricate stitching done by these little girls both charming and amazing. It was humbling to realize how very young these girls were when they stitched the samplers we were studying more than two centuries later. Inspired by their work, I designed a quilted version of a band sampler, substituting small-scale piecing and appliqué for cross-stitch and satin stitch. Adapting the motifs from several different English samplers was both a challenge and a pleasure. The resulting miniature quilt is one of my personal favorites, combining two much-loved styles of needlework—quilting and embroidery.

# Materials

½ yard of gold fabric for piecing, appliqué, and binding

½ yard of light pink fabric for piecing

½ yard of medium green fabric for piecing and appliqués

½ yard of light fabric for appliqué background

⅜ yard of light blue fabric for piecing and appliqués

¼ yard of dark green fabric for vines and leaves

1 fat quarter of dark blue fabric for piecing and appliqués

Scraps of assorted greens, pinks, blues, and golds for appliqués

⅝ yard of fabric for backing

16" x 29" piece of lightweight batting

## Accuracy Counts!

Remember—precision is very important for miniature quilts. Refer to "Cutting and Piecing" on page 6 and "Helpful Hints for Miniature Piecing" on page 66 for help cutting and sewing the pieced bands.

# Cutting

## Top and Bottom Pieced Bands

**From the medium green fabric, cut:**

8 strips, 1" x 12"

**From the light blue fabric, cut:**

4 strips, 1" x 12"

**From the gold fabric, cut:**

19 squares, 2" x 2"; cut each square twice diagonally to yield 76 triangles

## Center Pieced Band

**From the light blue fabric, cut:**

2 bias strips, 1¼" x 12"

**From the medium green fabric, cut:**

2 bias strips, 1¼" x 12"

**From the gold fabric, cut:**

7 squares, 2½" x 2½"; cut each square twice diagonally to yield 28 triangles (2 are extra)

## Sunshine and Shadow Bands

**From the medium green fabric, cut:**

18 strips, ⅞" x 12"

**From the gold fabric, cut:**

13 strips, ⅞" x 12"

**From the light blue fabric, cut:**

7 strips, ⅞" x 12"

**From the dark blue fabric, cut:**

2 strips, ⅞" x 12"

**From the light pink fabric, cut:**

30 strips, ⅞" x 12"

## *Appliqué Bands*

**From the light background fabric, cut:**

1 rectangle, 3¼" x 13½"

1 rectangle, 5" x 13½"

1 rectangle, 7½" x 13½"

1 rectangle, 3½" x 13½"

---

## *Helpful Hints for Miniature Piecing*

- Before cutting, press fabrics with spray starch to give them more body. The crisper the fabric, the easier it will be to work with.

- Make sure your rotary cutting blade is really sharp. A dull blade causes the fabric layers to shift more during cutting.

- Cut strips for minis along the lengthwise grain, parallel to the selvage edge. They will be more stable and less stretchy than strips cut crosswise, which will make them easier to piece accurately. Do not cut strips longer than 14".

- Use a fresh machine needle made for light-weight fabrics, size 70/10, and fine 60-weight thread so the seams will lie flatter.

- Sew with either a quilter's quarter-inch foot or a straight-stitch presser foot.

- If you have one, use a straight-stitch throat plate on your sewing machine. This plate will prevent stitch distortion due to small pieces of fabric being pushed down into the larger hole of a zigzag throat plate.

- Make a ¼" seam guide for your machine referring to "Sewing Accurate Seams" on page 7. Sew a test seam to check for accuracy.

- Use a stiletto or small screwdriver to help guide small pieces under the presser foot.

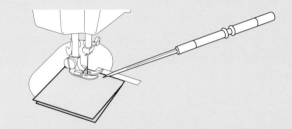

- Chain piece wherever possible.

- *Always press each seam in a strip set before adding another strip to the set.* Use spray starch to give the completed strip sets a final pressing before crosscutting them. The starch will give the small crosscut segments extra body, making them easier to handle.

- To reduce bulk, trim seams to ⅛" after sewing.

# Piecing the Top and Bottom Bands

1. Use the blue and green 1" x 12" strips to make four strip sets as shown. Trim seams to ⅛" and press seam allowances toward the green strips.

Make 4 strip sets.

2. Crosscut the strip sets into 38 segments, 1" wide.

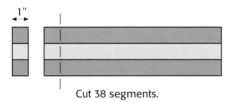

Cut 38 segments.

3. Sew a gold setting triangle on each end of each segment. Press the seams toward the green. Make 38.

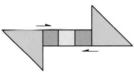

Make 38.

4. Sew 19 units together, as shown, to make the top pieced band. Trim seam allowances and press them in one direction. Repeat to make an identical pieced band for the bottom.

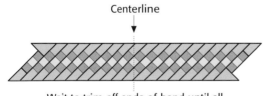

Centerline

Wait to trim off ends of band until all sampler's horizontal bands have been set together.

### Trim Later
Wait to trim off the ends of the pieced bands until all the horizontal panels have been set together.

# Piecing the Center Band

1. Sew one blue and one green 1¼" bias strip together along the long bias edges. Trim the seam allowance and press toward the green fabric. Make two bias strip sets.

2. Use a Bias Square ruler or a 1¼" square plastic template to mark twelve 1¼" bias squares on the joined strips as shown.

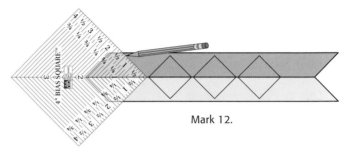

Mark 12.

3. Cut out the bias squares carefully, cutting exactly on the line.

4. Sew a gold setting triangle to each side of a bias square as shown. Press toward the bias square. Make 12.

Make 12.

5. Sew the bias square units together, as shown, to make the center pieced band. Add a gold triangle to each end as shown.

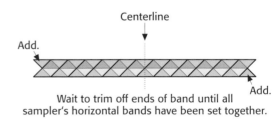

Centerline

Add.

Add.

Wait to trim off ends of band until all sampler's horizontal bands have been set together.

6. Trim the band to ¼" beyond the points of the squares on the top and bottom. Do not trim the sides yet.

# Assembling and Finishing the Quilt

1. Follow the diagram to lay out the pieced and appliquéd bands. Match and pin the centers of the bands carefully. The pieced bands will extend beyond the appliqué ends on the sides. Do not trim the ends of the pieced bands yet.

Assembly Diagram
Do not trim sides of quilt
until quilting has been completed.

2. Sew the bands together. Press all seam allowances toward the appliqué bands.

3. Cut a piece of quilt backing fabric, 15" x 27". Cut a piece of lightweight batting the same size as the backing fabric.

4. Layer the quilt top, batting, and backing together and baste through all layers. Baste carefully all around the edges (still untrimmed) of the quilt top.

5. Quilt as desired, by hand or machine, taking care not to stretch the outside edges as you quilt.

6. When quilting is complete, trim the quilt to measure 13" x 25". Machine stay stitch around the outer edges of the quilt top, stitching through all layers with a ⅛" seam allowance.

7. Using the remaining gold fabric, cut 1⅝"-wide bias strips for a narrow, double-fold bias binding. Bind the quilt, referring to "Binding" on page 18 for details if needed.

# Appliqué Patterns

Strawberries and Hearts Band

Strawberry Band

**Appliqué Patterns
and Placement Guide**
Leaf and Flower Band

# Somerset Swirl

*Made by Elizabeth Hamby Carlson, 1999*

Finished quilt: 26½" x 26½"

*While visiting* Wells Cathedral in Somerset, England, some brightly patterned floor tiles in the Lady Chapel caught my attention. Architectural elements are a rich resource for quilt design, and these Victorian tiles called out to be made into a quilt. I knew right away I wanted to use the lovely reproductions of fabric by Victorian designer William Morris for this small quilt.

I teach various methods of hand appliqué using the Somerset Swirl pattern, but this pattern is also suitable for machine appliqué. I like the simple design as a wall hanging, but it would make a terrific center medallion for a much larger quilt. One of these days I'll get started on that.

# Materials

1⅛ yards of pink-and-green print for appliqué, borders, and binding

⅞ yard of light fabric for appliqué background

¼ yard of dark green fabric for inner border

¼ yard or 1 fat quarter of medium green fabric for appliquéd vines and stems

Scraps of assorted pinks and greens for appliquéd flowers and leaves

⅞ yard of fabric for backing

32" x 32" piece of batting

# Cutting

**From the light background fabric, cut:**

1 square, 15½" x 15½"

2 squares, 12" x 12", cut once diagonally to make 4 triangles

**From the dark green fabric, cut:**

2 strips, 1" x 20½"

2 strips, 1" x 21½"

**From the pink-and-green print, cut:**

2 strips, 3¼" x 21½"

2 strips, 3¼" x 27"

# Appliqué

Refer to "Appliqué" on page 8 for appliqué methods and techniques, or use your own favorite method.

1. Fold the 15½" background square in quarters and press lightly to mark the centerlines. Fold diagonally and press to mark the diagonal lines.

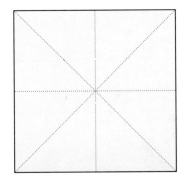

2. Use the appliqué pattern on page 78 to appliqué the center block. Sew the stems first, in alphabetical order. Leave approximately ½" free at the beginning of each stem section so the adjacent section can be tucked underneath it. Sew the free end after the adjacent section has been sewn.

3. Appliqué the remaining pieces in numerical order. When sewing the center swirl, leave the left edge of piece 1 free so that piece 8 can be tucked underneath it. Sew the left edge of piece 1 last to complete the swirl.

4. Trim and square up the center block to measure 14½" x 14½". Refer to "Squaring Up Blocks" on page 7.

5. Fold each of the four 12" background triangles in half in both directions to find the centerlines.

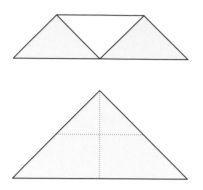

6. Using the corner appliqué pattern on page 77, appliqué each triangle. Sew the stems first, in alphabetical order, and then the remaining pieces in numerical order.

# Assembling the Quilt

1. Center two corner triangles on opposite sides of the center square and sew. Press the seam allowances toward the corner triangles.

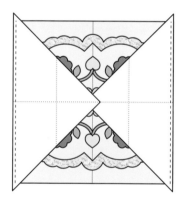

2. Sew corner triangles on the remaining two sides of the center square. Press the seam allowances toward the corner triangles.

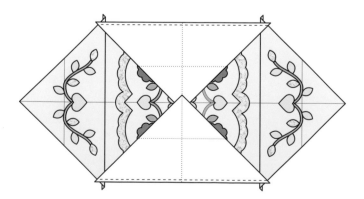

3. Trim and square up the center of the quilt to measure 20½" x 20½".

4. Sew the green 1" x 20½" inner-border strips to opposite sides of the quilt. Press the seam allowances toward the inner border.

5. Add the green 1" x 21½" inner-border strips to the top and bottom of the quilt. Press the seam allowances toward the inner border.

6. Sew the pink-and-green outer borders to the quilt in the same manner. Press the seams toward the inner border.

# Finishing the Quilt

Refer to "Finishing" on page 17 for detailed instructions if needed.

1. Center the quilt top and batting over the backing, and baste through all layers.

2. Quilt as desired, by hand or machine.

3. Trim the excess backing and batting. Cut the binding fabric into 2½"-wide bias strips. Sew the binding to the quilt.

4. Make a hanging sleeve and sew it to the quilt, if you wish, and add a label.

**Appliqué Patterns**

**Appliqué Patterns and Placement Guide**

15

10

11

14

13

B

A

12

2

3

1

4

9 Center

8

5

7

6

Beck, Thomasina. *Gardening with Silk and Gold: A History of Gardens in Embroidery.* Devon, England: David and Charles, 1997.

Carlson, Elizabeth Hamby. *Small Wonders: Tiny Treasures in Patchwork and Appliqué.* Woodinville, Washington: Martingale & Company, 1999.

———. *Trip to Ireland: Quilts Combining Two Old Favorites.* Woodinville, Washington: Martingale & Company, 2002.

———. *Burgoyne Surrounded: A Classic Quilt plus Six Variations.* Woodinville, Washington: Martingale & Company, 2004.

Dietrich, Mimi. *Happy Endings: Finishing the Edges of Your Quilt.* Woodinville, Washington: That Patchwork Place, 1987.

Johnson, Linda. *Pink Lemonade and Other Delights.* Woodinville, Washington: Martingale & Company, 2001.

Mahoney, Nancy. *Rich Traditions: Scrap Quilts to Paper Piece.* Woodinville, Washington: Martingale & Company, 2002.

Makhan, Rosemary. *Floral Abundance: Appliqué Designs Inspired by William Morris.* Woodinville, Washington: Martingale & Company, 2000.

Martin, Terry. *Fast Fusible Quilts: Cross-Stitch Quilts Made Easy.* Woodinville, Washington: Martingale & Company, 2001.

Weissman, Judith Reiter and Wendy Lavitt. *Labors of Love: America's Textiles and Needlework, 1650–1930.* New York, New York: Knopf, 1987.

Wilson, Erica. *Crewel Embroidery.* New York, New York: Charles Scribner's Sons, 1962.

Since making her first quilt in 1978, Elizabeth Hamby Carlson has made more quilts than she can count and always has at least a dozen more in the planning stages. She began teaching quiltmaking in 1983 and especially enjoys sharing her methods for hand appliqué, machine piecing, and miniature quiltmaking. Through her pattern business, Elizabeth Quilts, she markets original quilt patterns reflecting her interest in the decorative arts and quilting traditions of the eighteenth and nineteenth centuries. *Strawberry Fair* is her fourth book for Martingale & Company. Her award-winning quilts have been featured in numerous quilt publications, and she has appeared on HGTV's *Simply Quilts*.

In addition to her traditional quilts, Elizabeth, a lifelong Anglophile, also designs and makes quilts inspired by her interest in English history.

Raised in northeastern Ohio, Elizabeth lives with her husband in Montgomery Village, Maryland. She has a grown son and daughter, both of whom have lots of quilts. When Elizabeth is not quilting, she enjoys reading, antiquing, and planning her next trip to England.